AN APPROACH TO THE STUDY OF THE QUR'AN

BY

SIR NIZAMAT JUNG

KITAB BHAVAN
New Delhi-110002

Kitab Bhavan
Publishers, Distributors, Exporters & Importers
1784, Kalan Mahal, Darya Ganj
New Delhi-110002 (India)

Phone : (91-11) 3277392/93, 3274686
Web Site : www.kitabbhavan.com
E-mail : nasri@vsnl.com
Fax : (91-11) 3263383

ISBN : 81-7151-033-7
Code No. : A00001

Edition 1992
Edition 2001

Published in India by:
Nusrat Ali Nasri for Kitab Bhavan
1784, Kalan Mahal, Darya Ganj
New Delhi-110002 [India]

Printed in India at:
Nice Printing Press
Khureji Khas, Delhi-110051

CONTENTS

AN APPROACH TO THE STUDY OF THE QUR'AN

CHAPTER I

The Book and the Man

IN studying the Qur'an in my later years, I have realised the importance of finding a direct and intelligible line of approach to the heart of the message contained in it. The path of the reader has to be made smoother and easier than it has hitherto been under the guidance of learned commentators of the old school. For, it may be said without disrespect that those who professed deep knowledge of it seem to have often gone a little off the field—some of them indeed having soared away into the clouds of metaphysical dissertation, leaving their disciples bewildered on the earth below. We must not forget that the Qur'an was revealed for man's guidance, that it purports to be a clear guidance, and that the guidance it offers is essentially of a moral nature. Hence its claim to be *a book of practical wisdom for the improvement of man's conduct in life.*

If we approach it in this belief, our progress through it would be easier, our acquisition of knowledge more helpful, and its effect upon the mind more invigorating. My object in these pages is to suggest this mode of approach.

This essay is no more than a collection of notes made by me from time to time, which I have now put together and arranged in order.

The method I followed in studying the Qur'an was not that favoured by the learned; nor was it influenced by any desire to discover the esoteric significance of the Quranic message. The question ever present to my mind was only this: How did it come about that this one book, through the agency of one man, had so large a

The Book

share in shaping the destiny of the human race, and what was the nature of the miracle by which it could teach the savages of Arabia in the brief space of a few years to take their place in history as a righteous and powerful nation, and what was the secret of this nation-building power?

Pivot of Islamic Teaching

I have been reading the Qur'an diligently for the past 20 years, and if I was asked what my impression of its teaching was, I would say 'insistence on faith and righteous practice in all the concerns of life'. It exhorts man in the name of his Creator to purify the spirit by unceasing vigilence over his desires and actions; for whatever he does will affect his soul. Good makes it good, and evil makes it evil, and good and evil are their own requital. This maxim which has been repeated in the Qur'an over and over again, may be said to be the pivot of Islam; which further to reinforce, it has been laid down that none can take over the burden of another. This makes it quite clear to us that no soul can hope to get rid of its responsibility by passing it on to another, and that there is no room in Islam for such a doctrine as that of vicarious redemption.

In reading the Qur'an, I feel that the scene is laid in the midst of human life and human relations. The doings of the inhabitants of the small town of Mecca raised the big question of right and wrong, of true and false, of one God and many gods, of the permanent and indestructible and the transient and self-destroying. The quarrel of parties and the petty facts incident to it led to a clear perception in one great mind of what should be adopted, and what should be rejected. And this perception led it on by degrees to a recognition of universal truths and an unalterable faith in practical righteousness.

The lessons taken from everyday life thus led to the promulgation of an ethical code which was sanctified as religion by that exalted form of inspiration which is known as Revelation. All this is reflected in the pages of the Qur'an.

The Man

I am seated before the Ka'aba writing this, and I see that solid square building (around which hundreds of men and women are moving in 'Tawaf') as the centre of the great controversy which raged 1,370 years ago between the false and the true. There were idols within its walls then, bearing different names to which various divine powers were attributed and worship accorded. These attributes and powers were admitted by all except one man whose common sense told him that stocks and stones were not worthy of reverence! And something within him assured him that the Power which created Nature with all its diversity was in reality one indivisible omnipotent power, all-seeing and all-knowing and all-compelling. He was a man who had spent the best years of his youth in gazing upon Nature: upon earth and sky, and upon mountains and plains where clouds and showers brought forth herbs and plants to sustain the life of man, bird and beast. This suggestive view of Nature had been filling his mind with visions and with wonder; and the ever-recurring question from within the depths of his soul was, 'Who is the Maker of all this and the Ruler of all this?' Not those Idols sitting in the Ka'aba, surely! He continued to ponder until the chief actor in the visible scene of life, man, engaged the attention of this born observer of Nature. How was man generated? Was he self-created? What gave him his superiority? Did not the hand of man make those idols which he foolishly began to worship afterwards? How helpless, how contemptible those idols were! To think that they were the makers of this wonderful Universe! How absurd! How mad!

The mind of this man, deeply agitated night and day, brooding over this palpable untruth amidst the baffling problems of life, was shaken to its very depths, and he was lost for days in meditation and reverie. And often seeking solitude as a means to inspiration, he spent weeks in lonely mountain caves. Such were the preliminary conditions under which the future Prophet was being prepared for his Mission. He was haunted by a sense of the unreality of the life that prevailed among the inhabitants of Mecca with their false creed and depraved practices; and the reality of the great world of being which was governed by Divine Ordinance, of which he witnessed unmistakable signs on the earth around him and in the skies above, weighed upon him from hour to hour, from day to day. Thus his convictions grew deeper and stronger, but he could not express them—could not even mention them to any one. All that was surging up from within was forced back upon itself and increased the travail of his spirit, till there came the supreme moment in his life when he felt that he was an instrument in the hands of a mighty Power which was driving him on and urging him with an irresistible force to deliver to mankind the message of life and death, of salvation and perdition.

How he first received the formal Command, how with fear and trembling he first ventured to mention it to his beloved wife, and afterwards to some near relatives who soon became converts, and how, finally, he disclosed his Mission to the people of Mecca—to be jeered at and reviled and persecuted—all this is too well known to be repeated. Nor need we dwell upon the harrowing details of the cruelty which pursued him for no less than 10 or 11 years and made him an outlaw whose life was forfeit.

It is related that the people of Mecca who made life almost impossible for the Prophet tried to entice him by offering to him in marriage the most beautiful woman in Mecca and making him their king! Would he accept this or prefer to ruin himself by persisting in his mad pursuit? History has recorded his answer and its result.

Here we have a man who had no fear in him because he was all truth, who knew neither doubt nor despair, and whom the bitterest persecution could not make impatient or put out of temper, and whom no bribe could tempt. What was the secret of his fearlessness, his burning sincerity and his indomitable assurance? What but the truth of his mission as he felt it, the direct Command of God to exhort and guide mankind—a Command that must be obeyed. He felt that he was a vessel into which the voice of God, thrilling with His mighty power was being poured, and that his function was merely to deliver it to his fellow beings. The divine afflatus was utterly irresistible, and he could not suppress it. It was not he who was making use of it, but it was this afflatus which was making use of him! Like one of those receivers which receive and emit sounds, he was a mere passive agent; and the state in which he received and delivered his message has been compared to an epileptic fit! Such are the outstanding facts of his mission, and they are uncontroverted. What do they prove? That he was not a fabricator, that he was not a maker of books—that he was not a preacher of sermons. An illiterate man, unread and untaught (in the usual sense of the word), a man who had never been known to utter an untruth—such he stood before his people, and such he stands before the world: the deliverer of a saving message, the mouthpiece of a mighty voice, the instrument of Revelation. But this is only one aspect of him, the other is that of warner and moral preceptor. From this he becomes a reformer, a leader, a statesman, a nation-builder! And incidentally, as it were, he becomes also a legislator, a military commander and a king of men (in fact though not in name). And over and above and around all this is seen the halo of Prophethood, the insignia of Divine Ordinance. He was made to see visions as are not seen by ordinary beings, to utter prophecies of coming events, such as are beyond the utmost reach of human prevision. With such faculties and such powers, what was his actual work in life? *Moral guidance along the path of noble achievement*. This is the real message of the Qur'an of which he is the accredited exponent.

I began by saying that the essence of Quranic teaching was moral righteousness, and now I come to that stage in his career when he stands forth as the great teacher of practical righteousness showing how within a comparatively short period a community of cruel, wicked people, who owned no conscience within and no overruling power above, was subjugated and reformed so completely as to produce godly men fit to be his companions through life—men who proved capable of leading armies and administering conquered territories, yet who were contented with a private life of stern self-denial. The first Caliph had given away all his wealth at the very outset to serve the cause of Islam and lived like a poor man when he was at the head of affairs. When he sent forth armies his orders to the commanders were :—

'Remember, that you are always in the presence of God, on the verge of death, in the assurance of judgment, and the hope of paradise. Avoid injustice and oppression, consult with your brethren, and study to preserve the love and confidence of your troops. When you fight the battles of the Lord acquit yourselves like men, without turning your backs; but let not your victory be stained with the blood of women or children. Destroy no palm trees, nor burn any fields of corn. Cut down no fruit trees, nor do any mischief to cattle, only such as you kill to eat. When you make any covenant or article stand to it, and be as good as your word.'

What but the teachings of the Qur'an and the example of the great Prophet could have produced such a man, and later, a man like the great Omar, who, seated on the floor of the Prophet's Mosque at Medina in his patched clothes, could issue mandates to the Governors of Persia and Syria and Egypt to administer their charge like upright men, to live as simple godfearing men, to allow free access to all suppliants, not to have guards at their gates, not to wear silken garments, and so on? What but the teachings of the Qur'an and the example of the great Prophet could have produced commanders and soldiers who would not look with the eyes of desire on the spoils of Persia and the fabulous treasures of Madain? Can history show any other such instance of moral reform brought about by the personal influence of one man, or point to another such system of life expanding automatically into a great civilisation conspicuous by its durability? Is it not because of his unique personality and his unique work that Europe is lost in wonder at his achievement and that some Europeans are wishing in this twentieth century of false progress and impending disaster for the advent of a Dictator like Muhammad? We know what Carlyle, the man of deep thought and truthful soul and the hater of all sham, has said of him, and we know what Doctor Johnson, another sincere godfearing soul, has written about the Prophet's heart-burning cry which has been ringing in deserts and cities and palaces to lead men towards light.

The Quran: Nature's Book

The words of the Qur'an which were poured into the heart of the Prophet, reveal to us the soul of the man and the life of the man and the whole work of the man. They reveal also the scene amidst which he had to work—the fierce conflict, the bitter opposition and the assurance of final triumph. All this makes the Qur'an a human-book, as an English lady-friend of mine once remarked to me; and throughout its pages there runs a vein of virile common sense, and there is such convincing reasonableness in its simple arguments that it may well be called what another English friend of mine called it, a rational book.

It is a book of simple injunctions and prohibitions, direct in its appeal and reasonable in its statements, containing threats of punishment for bad, and promises of reward for good actions in this life, and giving fairly comprehensive lists of good and bad qualities. The language is simple, but it rises into fervid eloquence charged with thunder and music as the occasion may require. It is not a book to be easily ignored even by the apathetic. It is like a trumpet call to moral action—the pre-requisite of righteous living; and fortunately for us there is no unintelligible metaphysics in it, no incomprehensible mystery.

By saying all this, it is not my intention to convey that the Qur'an is anything like a well arranged text-book dividing its subject-matter into sections following a logical order. No such thing. On the contrary it may be said to be, as some European writers have actually said, a jumble! And this to my mind is the most convincing proof of its not having been deliberately written by man! It is a collection of spontaneous messages uttered under some strong compulsive pressure, consisting partly of exclamations and exhortations, and threats and promises, and partly of observations and reflections on the fate of races which perished in their contumacy after having rejected the warnings sent to guide and save them. It gives a brief account, in different chapters, of the Missions of Moses and Jesus and other Prophets. The chief characteristic of the Book is that it is interspersed throughout with directions concerning righteous conduct and propriety of behaviour, while it contains specific laws governing conjugal relations and inheritance and charity, etc. The style of the shorter chapters revealed at Mecca is, generally speaking, abrupt and exclamatory and elliptical. Pictures are flashed upon the mind by pointing to certain signs in Nature as tokens of God's power and providence, in the face of which man persists in his ingratitude. Observation of Nature, strong feelings aroused by it, sudden intuitions of abiding truths, thrilling impulses—all these combined in a mysterious manner and made the utterer a passive vocal instrument.

The Cry of The Prophet

This accounts for the style of the Qur'an and its apparent disorder which is so confusing to those who are unable to follow the inner movements of the Prophet's mind and its perplexities and the over-powering influence operating upon it. It explains the nature of the 'Cry of the Prophet'. This happy phrase of Dr. Johnson's is like a ray of light falling upon a dark place and stultifies all that jargon about the jumble. As there is unity in

Nature's diversity, one power running through and giving life to everything, so there is a unity of theme and thought and feeling running through the apparently ill-arranged subject-matter of the Qur'an. Readers used to well-arranged books and unused to Prophets' cries must naturally be repelled by the Qur'an at first sight, but let them go on reading and re-reading it till the spell begins to work and the sounds of the words and the sights they reveal carry them off into a world above perception—a world in which there is an intuitive recognition of reality. It is then that the pictures become vivid and enlarged till they overspread heaven and earth, and the sounds swell into that thunder-music which is not to be found in the language of any other book.

The attitude of the reader towards the Qur'an is not to be that of a critic sitting down with the avowed object of writing an article for a literary magazine, or a paragraph for the book-note column of a journal. Nor should it be that of a Doctor of Theology with a mind heavily laden with cumbersome learning and prepossessed in favour of some one system and prejudiced against all others. All sacred books have a natural appeal in them, and the appeal is to unsophisticated minds. Go to them with an open mind and a clean heart, and you will not fail to find something good in them—the spirit of good, at any rate. But, for the Qur'an, I claim something more than this, namely, an extraordinary breadth of vision, truth to nature, insistence on practical righteousness while teaching man to live according to nature. It insists on the separation of good from evil, of right from wrong. It brings religion down from the clouds and fixes it upon solid earth as a world-compelling power, even as Socrates is said to have done in regard to philosophy. It does not confine Nature within artificial bounds, it does not prescribe any ritual as being essential to salvation. The daily prayer it enjoins is not a 'ritual' but a remembrance and an acknowledgment of subordination and gratitude to the Creator, and of the very essence of it is the earnest desire to be guided aright. IT MAKES ALL MANKIND ONE BROTHERHOOD. It pronounces them to belong to one religion—the religion of Nature, the religion of voluntary and cheerful submission to the laws of Nature as promulgated by its God. Does not the law of Nature comprehend all creation? It is the universality of its teaching, the truth of its prophetic visions, and the lucidity and fervour of its simple language that give to the Qur'an that wonderful power which moves the heart and brings tears to the eyes. Its voice is, in truth, a ringing 'Prophet's cry'! Get rid of the notion that it is a text-book of sermons written for the pulpit, and you get rid of much false thinking about the Qur'an. Get rid also of the nebulous belief that it is the mystical language of heaven, above and beyond human comprehension, and you will find it a human book sent for human guidance in *this* life—*through* which lies the way to heaven or hell.

Mankind one Brotherhood

The voice of the Qur'an, I repeat, with all its music and its thunder is a clear call to moral action: an inspiriting, invigorating, reassuring call. There is no tremour of doubt or hesitancy in it anywhere, no trace of speculative uncertainty.

It exhorts man to rise to the full stature of completed manhood, so as to realise the divine element in his spirit. It proclaims his perfectability through righteous endeavour. It lays the foundation of his heaven in this very world of toil and strife. It encourages him to face the world as it is, to work in the midst of it, and to accept the facts of Nature as part of the great Scheme. He is neither to run away from them, nor to yield timidly to such as may be evil, but to combat them and overcome them and so save himself from their injurious effects. This is the Right Path.

The Qur'an makes the acceptance of the universal law the foremost duty of man. It teaches him to live in accord with it and seek and gain his balance as a sentient, rational, responsible being,—passion-driven but spiritually guided. Such submission to the divine order of things is Islam. It is the religion of Nature.

Is this not what man from the earliest stage of his existence has been trying to find? And is this not what the Stoic philosophers sought? And is this not what all the religions and all the philosophies that we know of came into the world to teach? And is this not what we really mean by such terms as civilization, culture, etc.,—that is, living up to the highest and best that man is capable of?

We Muslims believe implicitly in the divine origin of the Book and call it a Revelation; and we refuse to attach any importance at all to such 'critical' remarks as would apply more appropriately to books written by men.

The Qur'an, a Revelation

But people of other religions, who think and say that it was composed by the Prophet are confronted with a serious difficulty when they have to explain how it became possible for an illiterate Arab of the 7th century, who had not met any men of learning conversant with the literature and philosophy of civilized nations, to have taken such a deep and comprehensive view of the life of man and its vital needs, to have gone into such detail regarding the essentials of the good life, and to have crystalized the ethics of all systems into short pithy maxims of conduct in the form of practical injunctions and prohibitions? How is it that no other great writer of ancient or modern times has ever produced such a book, out of the teachings of which has arisen a new world of civilization and culture? In a word, how did it happen that this unlettered man could throw up from the depths of his mind words that are like sparks of light charged with soul-compelling sound, 'words that breathe and thoughts that burn'? We have either to take the Book as a Revelation, or the man himself as a Revelation.

Islam a complete civilization

And what did the Book and the man give to the world? 'Islam' which as Dr. Gibb says, 'is indeed much more than a system of theology; it is a complete civilization. If we were to seek for parallel terms, we should use Christendom rather than Christianity, China rather than Confucianism. It includes a whole complex of cultures which have grown up around the religious core, or have in most cases been linked on to it with more or less modification, a complex with distinctive features in political, social and economic structure, in its conception of law, in ethical outlook, intellectual tendencies, habits of thought and action. Further, it includes a vast number of peoples differing in race, language, character and inherited aptitudes, yet bound together not only by the link of a common creed, but even more strongly by their participation in a common culture, their obedience to a common law and their adoption of a common tradition.'*

*Extract from 'Whither Islam' edited by H. A. R. Gibb.

Religion for a commonwealth of Nations

Is not this a religion that can build up a commonwealth of nations on a firmer basis than that of political convention? Dr. Gibb continues: 'We are so accustomed to think of Islam as an oriental religion and of its culture as an oriental culture that we are apt to overlook the real character of Moslem civilization and to miss its true place and significance in the history of human society. The old view that Islam issued from Arabia in a complete, fixed, and unalterable form has long been recognized as a fallacious half-truth. Even in the narrow field of religious doctrine, Islam remained for at least two centuries relatively plastic. Its fundamental principles were doubtless fixed once and for all, but they were not finally developed into a theology until after a long period of controversy. Now the religion of Islam itself is a branch of that group of religions which includes also Zoroastrianism, Judaism, and Christianity and shares with them the same ultimate postulates. From the very first it belonged, in consequence, to what we may call—in contradistinction to the Indian and Chinese religious groups—the western group. This western character was, moreover, intensified in the sequel. The outer world into which Islam issued from Arabia was the Hellenistic world, the heir of Graeco-Roman civilization, and almost all its early conquests were made within this Hellenistic world. Thus it came about that the *external* influences which moulded Moslem civilization were Hellenistic and Persian. Its intellectual life was penetrated through and through by Greek culture; its very theology is in debt to Aristotle. The whole culture of Islam was thus essentially a culture of the western type, and stands much closer to us than the cultures of India and the Far East. To call it

" oriental " is a misnomer; it is oriental not in the absolute sense, but only in its local extension, as the eastern branch of western civilization, and it has at all times been shared by Jews and eastern Christians as well as Moslems.'

Does this not prove the breadth and elasticity of Islam, its capacity for adapting itself to its environments and absorbing into itself all that is best in the world's culture without departing from its essential principles or allowing their purity to be impaired?

This is the work of the man who stands out as the grandest figure in history.

Gibbon writes about his work:

Gibbon on Islam

'It is not the propagation but the permanency of his religion that deserves our wonder: the same pure and perfect impression which he engraved at Mecca and Medina is preserved, after the revolutions of twelve centuries, by the Indian, the African, and the Turkish proselytes of the Koran. If the Christian apostles, St. Peter or St. Paul, could return to the Vatican, they might possibly inquire the name of the Deity who is worshipped with such mysterious rites in that magnificent temple: at Oxford or Geneva, they would experience less surprise; but it might still be incumbent on them to peruse the catechism of the church, and to study the orthodox commentators on their own writings and the words of their master. But the Turkish dome of St. Sophia, with an increase of splendour and size, represents the humble tabernacle erected at Medina by the hands of Mahomet. The Mahometans have uniformly withstood the temptation of reducing the object of their faith and devotion to a level with the senses and imagination of man. " I believe in one God, and Mahomet the apostle of God," is the simple and invariable profession of Islam. The intellectual image of the Deity has never been degraded by any visible idol; the honours of the prophet have never transgressed the measure of human virtue; and his living precepts have restrained the gratitude of his disciples within the bounds of reason and religion.'*

Leitner's tribute to Islam

The following extracts from an Essay on Muhammadanism by G. W. Leitner, written more than 50 years ago, would further help to elucidate what I have said:

Approach to another's Religion

'It really seems to me that if men cultivated something like true charity they would have a different view of other religions than they now hold, and that they would endeavour to learn about them from their original sources, instead of from the prejudiced second-hand reports of the opponents of these religions.'

To walk with God is practice in Islam

'"To walk with God", to have God with us in our daily life with the object of obtaining the "peace that passeth all understanding", to submit "to the Divine will" — this we, too, profess to seek; but in Muhammadanism this profession is translated into practice, and is the corner-stone of the edifice of that faith.'

* * * * *

'In one sense Muhammadanism is like, and in another sense unlike, both Judaism and Christianity. To walk with God, to have God ever present in all our acts, is no doubt what the prophets of these religions taught; and

* *Decline and Fall of the Roman Empire*, ch. L., pp. 282-283.

in that sense they were all Muhammadans, or rather "Muslims"—namely, professors of the faith of "Islam".'

* * * * *

'But so far as I know anything either of Judaism or of Christianity, the system preached by Muhammad was not merely imitative or eclectic; it was also "inspired"—if there be such a process as inspiration from the source of all goodness. Indeed, I venture to state in all humility that if self-sacrifice, honesty of purpose, unswerving belief in one's mission, a marvellous insight into existing wrong or error, and the perception and use of the best means for its removal, are among the outward and visible signs of inspiration, the mission of Muhammad was "inspired".'

Muhammad Was Inspired

* * * * *

'The idea of Muhammad not to limit the benefits of Abraham's religion to his own people, but to extend them to the world, has thus become the means of converting to a high form of culture and of civilisation millions of the human race, who would either otherwise have remained sunk in barbarism, or would not have been raised to that brotherhood which "Islam" not only preaches but also practises.'

Islam's Universality

* * * * *

'It seems to me that the question of what Muhammadanism really is cannot be summed up better than in stating it to be pure Judaism plus proselytism, and original Christianity minus the teaching of St. Paul. This as regards its theory; in practice it is far more than modern Christianity in its artificial European aspect—the "Sermon on the Mount" translated into daily life.'

* * * * *

'Nowhere in Muhammadan society is there any invidious distinction between rich and poor; and even a Muhammadan slave is not only a member of the household, but has also far greater chances of rising to a position in the Government or in society than an English pauper.'

Freedom and Equality

*   *   *   *   *

There would be no Nihilists and no Socialists in Europe were Western society constituted on the basis of Muhammadanism; for in it a man is not taught to be dissatisfied, as is the great effort, aim, and result of our civilisation.

*   *   *   *   *

'On the unlimited polygamy which produced this state of things Muhammad put a check; he directed that a man could only enter into the marriage contract with two, three, or four wives, if he could behave with equal justice and equal love to them all.

Polygamy

Unless he could do that he was only permitted to marry one wife. Now as, practically, no one can be, as a rule, equally fair and loving to two or more wives, the spirit of Muhammad's legislation is clearly in favour of monogamy.'

'I believe that the real cause of his many marriages at an old age was charity, and in order to protect the widows of his persecuted followers.'

*   *   *   *   *

'He also raised woman from the condition of being a property to that of a proprietor; and he constituted her as the first "legal" sharer whose interests the Muhammadan law has to consult.'

Status of Woman

*   *   *   *   *

'The married woman is in a better legal position than the married English woman, and she can give evidence in attestation of a birth, marriage, or death, which is still denied to a woman in Republican France.'

* * * * *

Islam's Moral Standard

'The Muhammadans have no taverns, gaming houses, or brothels, nor have they any idea of legalising prostitution; and as regards their general conversation it is infinitely more decent, as a rule, than that of most Europeans. I have seen young Muhammadan fellows at school and college, and their conduct and talk are far better than is the case among English young men indeed, the talk of the latter is often such as would incur punishment in a Muhammadan land.'

Meaning of Holy War

'As regards the assumed immutability of the Muhammadan religion, there is a liberty of interpretation of the Koran which enables "Islam" to be adapted to every sect and country, e.g. the law laid down for its interpretation that conditional sentence has to take precedence of an absolute one, is one that secures every reasonable liberty of conscience: e.g., "fight the infidels" is an absolute sentence; "fight the infidels if they attack you first" is a conditional sentence, and has therefore first to be taken into account in determining the much misunderstood question of the "Holy war" or rather "Jihad", against infidels. Indeed, no such war is legitimate except in self-defence against those who persecute Muhammadans because they believe in one God and who turn them out from their homes; in other words, as in the case of the Muslim refugees to Abyssinia.'

* * * * *

'As for religious toleration, there is much more of it in practice among Muhammadans than has been the case, at any rate, in Christian countries; and had this not been the fact, the Armenian, Greek, and Jewish communities would not have preserved their autonomy, religion, and language under, say, Turkish rule—a rule, I may add from personal knowledge—which offers many lessons of forbearance and humanity to Christian legislation.'

Tolerance in Islam

* * * * *

'Muhammad included Jews and Christian among Muslims; or those who believe in God and the last day "shall have no fear upon them, neither shall they grieve".'

Kinship with Christianity, Judaism

'I cannot conclude this address better than by insisting on the fact that the Jewish, Christian, and Muhammadan religions are sister-faiths, having a common origin; and by expressing a hope that the day will come when Christians will honour Christ more by also honouring Muhammad.

'There is a common ground between Muhammadanism and Christianity, and he is a better Christian who reveres the truths enunciated by the Prophet Muhammad.'

CHAPTER II

Islam Misrepresented

Religion and Bigotry

IT makes one sad to think that some of our religious people professing to be exponents of the teachings of the Qur'an show, not only narrow-mindedness and intolerance at times, but also carelessness of truth and sincerity. A sense of false superiority arising from supposed orthodoxy, a punctilious observance of the ritual of religion and some of its negligible details relating chiefly to costume and ablution, and an arrogant assumption that they alone will be saved—all these seem to turn their thoughts away from the essentials of religion, which are truth, sincerity, purity of heart, in one word, righteousness.

Some of these sanctimonious gentlemen consider it their foremost religious duty to consign the followers of all other religions straightway to perdition. Their conception of the Deity seems to be not mercy, benevolence and grace, but wrath and vengeance personified! They think more about the anger of God than about his kindness and mercy and never-ceasing grace. I cannot think of God as being angry because anger is a human, and purely animal passion, and God must be above it. His attributes must be those which are considered purest, highest and best in man, and that at the very highest and best. Anger and vengeance imply resentment, which in its nature is a personal feeling. Nothing that God does is personal to him, however personal it may be to us. His will, His judgment, and His deed are all one, and they are Universal Law. And in that Law are Justice and Mercy and Grace to crown Retribution.

This is the impression I get from reading the Qur'an. It gives the essence of the divine to us in a human guise; and the language used is that of a kind father admonishing and warning his truant children in order to guide them back to the right path. There are passages in it here and there, the pathetic benevolence and divine humanity of which brings tears to our eyes. And the wonder of it all is, that it is the plain and simple language of reason, though occasionally metaphorical, and the object of it is guidance of mankind by indicating the essential everlasting distinction between good and evil, between right and wrong. It does not inspire terror, but hope with its expectancy of bliss; and it purifies and confirms faith.

It is an erroneous belief—mostly inculcated by narrow-minded bigotry—that the Qur'an condemns the followers of all other religions to eternal perdition as 'Kafirs'. It does not unconditionally; it shows a kindly feeling towards Christians, and even as regards Jews it readily makes benevolent exceptions in favour of good ones. It ever stresses the fact that all men will be judged in accordance with what they have earned by their deeds. 'Kafirs' in the Quranic sense are only those who are persistent polytheists and refuse to believe in the unity of God and the mission of the Prophet. Far from such denial it necessarily follows that their conception of the universe and of the inter-relation of all the powers and the existences in it is utterly perverse. It destroys the oneness of being and the universality of divine law. Before a God who represents these and is the Paramount Power, the small Deities of Polytheism must appear as traitors and usurpers, and their votaries as seditionists and rebels! Is there any injustice in this?

And yet the Qur'an enjoins forbearance towards other religions and persuasions however false they may be. 'Do not abuse others' religion for they may retort by saying things against Allah.'

Sectarian Prejudice against the Qur'an

Experience teaches us that learning does not necessarily release the mind from prejudice; and it is a well-known fact that the human mind can always find arguments for proving what it wishes to believe. It is an adept in chasing and capturing mendacious arguments for its own purposes, and once it begins to follow the scent, it is so intent on the trail, that it fails to see the true arguments lying under its very nose! This may be a reflection upon the attitude of learned writers of commentaries on the Qur'an who only succeed in making obscure what was transparently clear, and it may be a reflection on the lucubrations of some of the foreign scholars (or scholiasts) who have felt a call to write about the Qur'an and the Founder of Islam. From beneath the deliberately superimposed calm of apparently dispassionate and austerely impartial critical judgment, some of them seem to emit occasional sparks of ill-suppressed anger and ill-concealed malice. Open any introduction to any translation of the Qur'an at any page at hazard, and you will observe some little sign of this. In some cases you come across a very carefully designed piece of literary workmanship heavy with unexpressed thoughts, the reservations of which are of portentous significance. It is sometimes difficult to understand what they mean to convey.

It has been alleged by some that Muhammad cannot be regarded as a prophet of truth in the absolute meaning of the term! One wonders what is truth in its absolute meaning.

The creed of Islam is so simple and so natural that it has no need to be propped up by any quasi-metaphysical doctrine of Neo-Platonic mysticism. There is only one God, Almighty, Just and Merciful, the Creator of all that is in the universe, and Muhammad is his Apostle, because he was His creature and instrument for conveying the message of the oneness and might and majesty, of the justice and mercy and benevolence of God. He delivered it to a world in which human beings were worshipping stocks and stones fashioned by their own hands into a semblance of divine idols. The message was delivered, it was willingly or unwillingly accepted, and within a few short years it transformed Arabia and laid the foundation of a new world of thought and action, and shaped the mould of a new Civilization. A great and glaring untruth was being accepted by the human mind under the name of religion in the guise of those uncouth, ill-fashioned images. One man saw the untruth of it all in its naked deformity and had the courage to proclaim it as such, and to fight against it till he destroyed it and replaced it with a simple and majestic truth: namely, that the unseen God is One and Eternal and Almighty. That man also had the courage to say to his countrymen: 'This is the truth and you shall believe it. I have been ordained by the Lord of Creation to convey it to the world, and I am therefore His chosen Messenger.' Is there any imposture in this, any false doctrine, any claim that was not justified by the whole life of the man?

The Qur'an is nothing if it does not convey this great moral and spiritual lesson to man: 'Thou must earn thy salvation by thy faith and thy good deeds alone; if thou doest good it is for thy own soul, if thou doest evil it is also for thy own soul, and thou shalt answer for it.'

The prophet of Islam was not trying to discover truths. Simple truths of a universal nature were being poured into his heart by the great Power that rules the Universe. His part was to have them believed and put into practice. No Prophet had ever done more than this.

The Prophet of Islam never professed to be introducing a new religion; neither did Jesus. They professed only to have been missioned to restore the old religion to its purity. The Qur'an is merely a confirmation of the divine message sent through Moses and Jesus; and Islam does not claim to be a new religion: it is a reassertion of the old faith in a less ambiguous form.

CHAPTER III

Revelation and Prophethood

THE words 'prophet' and 'revelation' suggest the question 'How does God reveal himself to man?' Through His works by means of an intuitive enlightenment. Even when there is direct communication between God and man, as in the case of revealed religions, can it be anything other than inspiration in the fullest and highest sense of the word? A message comes from somewhere to a human mind that is in a state of uncommon exaltation; it is breathed into it—'inspired', and 'reveals' certain truths to it. It is clothed in language, but that language is not quite the same as that of man's ordinary speech; it has sublimity in it, and a fire and a glow that are not usually within the compass of ordinary speech. It is poetic, it is prophetic, it is soulstirring and soul-exalting, and therefore capable in the highest degree of impressing the minds and thrilling the hearts of hearers.

The Holy Books have come to man in this way and this is the only way we can understand. For no one in these days would accept any statement that purported to convey the information that a book in a book form had come down ready-made from heaven, as from the publishers. Would any one suppose that the Almighty would consider it necessary to send His message in writing to such primitive pastoral people as the patriarchs and the early prophets? Our conception of revelation and prophecy is merely this: a great and irresistible wave of thought and emotion sweeps over the mind of the inspired man, the prophet, and brings to him the vision of a world more splendid and more perfect than this one. All his faculties are raised to the point of frenzy and he is under the domination of a mysterious power which he cannot resist, and his innermost belief all the while is that the message of salvation has come direct from God as a 'revelation' and must be delivered at once to his fellow beings.

Understood as inspiration, revelation admits of many degrees. It covers the whole range that lies between the advent of the holy books and the birth of any sudden good thought that comes to us in a flash and lights up the dark corners of the mind. And in the intervening space between these two lies the work of poets, and philosphers and sages and reformers, all of whom reveal truth and beauty to us in their own way and bring light and purity and sweetness into our earthly life.

Insight into Nature's Ways

Some men have a wonderful insight into Nature's ways, and her mysteries are revealed to them by some intuitive process. If their emotions are wrought into a state of ecstasy or frenzy by what they witness, they become poets and prophets; but if their natures are less highly strung, they remain mere passive spectators of those mysteries, lost in wonder and contemplation.

Such insight is a gift from Nature. It may be cultivated and rendered more acute and more active by constant use; but it cannot be acquired by any human means. A poet is born, not made; so is a prophet, so is a true philosopher or a sage. He comes into the world with his gift—though it may take years, perhaps more than half a life-time, before the gift is revealed even to his own inner consciousness. When it is revealed to him and to the world, he knows it as an accession of new power; but it was in him potentially from the very beginning of the Universe: Whatever we may call it on this earth, it is a ray of the divine, a reflex of some attribute of God, which is sometimes found in the most unexpected places.

Religion Revealed

Religion in the highest sense is that which brings to the human mind an intense conviction of the existence of a moral order in the Universe under the direction of a Supreme Being, and this without the aid of any dialectical process. Religion compels belief without any logical explanation, by simply appealing to some hidden faculty in us, which is not the same as understanding. Our cognizance of truth and response to it under the influence of religion is rather instinctive than intellectual; hence the mind does not require and does not rely on any process of philosophical investigation, though it may occasionally employ such a process to the extent that it may support and confirm its conclusions.

Belief in the existence of God may be said to be inherent in human nature, but it requires the authority of religion to give it a definite form so as to intensify its reality. And every religion that has come to man as a revelation may claim the authority of a divine command. And in the case of such religions it seems idle to question their divine origin, unless we be in a position to decide by what particular means, to the exclusion of all others, communication between God and man is made. Revelation, so far as we know, has been vouchsafed to one chosen man at a time and not simultaneously to all men of the same tribe or race; and that one man has been made the means of communicating it to his contemporaries. Revelation to him was no other than inspiration, something breathed into him or borne in upon him in such a way as to make utterly impossible any unbelief or doubt as to its divine origin. It was a sudden flash of light that pierced his soul through and through and enabled it to see the reality of being; it was as though a closed door had been opened suddenly to give him a glimpse of what lay on the other side in a region hitherto unseen. Any soul that aspires towards the real and eternal may have such brief moments of illumination when all that is dark seems lighted up by a radiance that comes from some unknown region. In ordinary life it generally takes the form of good impulses; in the case of genius it assumes some new and remarkable form; in the case of a seer it is something like second sight. In the case of a prophet, it is called Revelation on account of its lucid intensity and comprehensiveness and the universality of its essential truths. And the truths are made manifest in such an intelligible form that the mind of man readily assents to them. Such a truth for instance is the Unity and Omnipotence of God; and it is necessarily followed by the belief that what He does must be right, and that His directions if followed conscientiously will guide us aright in our life here and hereafter, and that our best course is to resign ourselves to His will by following His directions which lead us away from evil. Acting in this way, under a haunting sense of moral responsibility, is called righteousness. This is the teaching of Islam, and it came to the world through the medium of one man who for this reason is known to the world as the Prophet of Islam. It came to him through the highest and purest form of inspiration —known as Revelation.

Islam has two distinct advantages over the other great religions of the world—that of having been born in the full light of history, and that of having been given to the world in the form of an unalterable document. Hardly any other religion can claim the same definiteness, either in respect of its birth or of its content. And this is the chief reason why there is no mystery about Islam and why it has been so little liable to the illusive process of traditional mystification.

Islam Historic and Definite

Supervised by Providence, it was given to the world by being revealed in a very definite rational sense to a very definite human being who was neither a myth nor a shadowy God-man. It was sent right into the midst of two great empires bordering upon the land of its birth; it came into early conflict with them; it overcame both and completely absorbed one of them. It subjugated ancient kingdoms, not so much by its arms, as by the forceful vitality of its new culture. There is no mysterious haze surrounding it; it stands out before our eyes a clearly defined historic fact. And there is no mystery in its tenets because they rest upon three simple fundamental beliefs supported by reason. (I) The undoubtable supremacy of one Omnipotent Creator and Controller of all things, (II) His communication of vital truths to man through a chosen Messenger in the form of Revelation, (III) An intelligible Message rationally explained for the spiritual and moral guidance of man in his present life which is to continue in a purified state hereafter.

Here is a conception of religion too simple to admit of sacerdotal mystification. It brings faith within every man's reach and makes it acceptable through reason.

I. There is but one God, Omnipotent, Just and Merciful. Who can gainsay this without becoming an atheist or a polytheist?

II. He appoints Messengers and guides for directing man to the right path. Who can question the truth of this without setting aside all the prophets and teachers and leaders known to all the religions?

III. He sends an intelligible message for the moral and spiritual guidance of man. Who can contest this without dissociating morality from religion and thus making the latter useless?

To any one who recognizes the truth of all this, there can be no doubt as to the strength of the claim put forward for Islam on these general grounds. But it is conceivable that if such a person happened to be a non-Muslim, he might be inclined to question whether the great Prophet of Islam was a real prophet missioned by God. The answer to this would depend upon one's notion as to what a 'real prophet' is, with what qualities he is endowed, in what manner he appears and conducts his mission, what kind of message he conveys to mankind, and whence his impulse to action is derived.

Miracle not essential to Prophethood

If we sought only the strange and the supra-natural or extra-natural as an essential condition of real prophethood, then the greater the remoteness of any alleged fact from natural probability, the greater and more convincing would be the reality of a prophet's mission and status. Take for instance the ability to perform miracles. If this was taken to be the only criterion of prophethood, many good prophets would be disqualified and excluded on the ground that no specific miracles are recorded of them.

The faith in miracles is a curious incident of the human mind, somewhat in the nature of a self-contradiction. Though we are generally incredulous of the unnatural, yet we seem to demand at times the incredible as the only acceptable proof of power! Such is our attitude towards miracles. Consciously or unconsciously we argue that since man cannot ordinarily perform such acts, the man who can and does perform them must be more than man. And because we readily believe that the act alleged must have been performed, there is no need to ask for further evidence ; for, obviously, there can be no impossibility where the Omnipotence of God is concerned, from which the power of miracles is directly derived. Such is the reasoning of faith and no one has any right to quarrel with it.

Now let us take the case of a man whose power did not extend to the performance of miracles, or of whom miracles are either not recorded or not believed. If such a man conveyed great truths to mankind in a natural way under the overpowering influence of some inner impulse or inspiration soaring into the region of prophecy, would any sane judgment deny to him the same degree of credence as in the other case? Or would it be fair to let the Omnipotence behind the scene remain unacknowledged in his case?

What is the true Criterion

There may be yet another variety of prophethood, combining the miraculous with the reasonable, revealing an extraordinary agency as the source of inspiration, but at the same time disclaiming any status or function higher than that of man. Such is the case with the great Prophet of Islam. Divinely inspired through the medium of an angel, he behaves in every respect and speaks on all occasions as a man. He claims nothing divine for himself expect the message which he is commanded to deliver to mankind. The modesty of his claim makes a strong appeal to rational minds, and the intervention of an angel does not become an insuperable obstacle to faith. For even a 'rationalist' would perhaps hesitate to assert that there can be no angels and spirits. He could only say, and with truth, that neither he nor any of his friends or acquaintances had ever seen one! But this argument would not go very far, the real question being, whether the seer or prophet had seen one or not, whether the appearance to him was 'real' or not. Here we need not enter into the consideration of subjective and objective reality—terms which do not carry us beyond the limits of our own dialectics. To the idealist all is unreal; to the realist all is real. But apart from all this, have we not many recorded and verified instances of abnormal phenomena even in these modern times of science and scepticism, to which some of the most distinguished scientists of the day have accorded their assent? On these grounds, to many of us the intervention of an angel would be less incredible than the actual performance of an act purporting to suspend or materially alter the operation of the laws of Nature. The apparition of an angel may be conceded even by the sceptical to be a concrete presentment of that unknown agency which gives intensity to inspiration and exalts it to the height of revelation. To many of us this proposition is quite intelligible; and thus understood, it does not come into conflict with our regard for natural probability. Whether we give the name angel or inspiration or revelation to the means of communication, the fact remains that it is a 'state of consciousness' in its most intense and realistic form of activity. If the person brought under its influence should give to the world nothing substantial, nothing useful, but mere fancies and illusions, he would deserve to be suspected as a mere visionary; but if on the contrary, he should give to the world a simple and intelligible article of faith and an equally simple code of practical morality, and succeed in establishing an indissoluble link between faith in God and practical righteousness in life, such a man would naturally rank among the highest among mankind, a leader and benefactor. As a prophet, he reaches an uncommon elevation. Is there anything irrational in this?

European thought has a conception of something extraordinary in the human mind which it calls 'genius'—a state of extraordinary enlightenment that eludes psychological analysis. It has been known to exist in some men, and has been recognized by the nature and quality of their work. Granted that such a state of mind exists, is there any reason for questioning the existence of a more intensified form of 'enlightenment' to which the name 'Revelation' is not inappropriately given?

A careful reader of the Qur'an cannot possibly fail to note that revelation from above on which Muhammad's prophethood rests is no more than his enlightenment by the Eternal Mind for the guidance of mankind from darkness towards light. He is constantly reminded that he is a mere mortal, and only a warner; neither its guardian nor its protector. The Prophet himself insisted on his being a mortal like his audience; only that he was acting under divine guidance and had a universal message to deliver. His message is the whole of the Qur'an, and it is his warrant of authority which, as understood by his contemporaries and by posterity, contains matters far more vital, far more comprehensive and universal in their application than any miracle.

Following this rational line of thought, we get further and further away from the notion of the strange, the unnatural, the weird, the mystical, the portentous as furnishing the true test of prophethood. And it is necessary to get away as far from it as possible in order to understand rightly, and appreciate justly the true merits of Islam as a practicable religion.

I have roughly indicated the two modes of approach and the two poles of faith—the natural and the unnatural. If we are believers in the one, it is inevitable that we should have no faith in its opposite. I have also suggested another lying midway between these two extremes, a middle course for a more accommodating type of mind to follow. Such a mind taking even the strange and abnormal to be possible as a manifestation of Omnipotence, would in the main pursue the more intelligible sequence of events in its endeavour to arrive at intelligible faith.

The merely strange and abnormal cannot and ought not to be set up as a criterion by which we are to judge of the reality of the prophethood of Muhammad and the truth of his mission. The manifestations of divine power as vouchsafed to Moses and to Jesus ought not to be demanded as essential to the credibility of Islam; firstly, because so little that is historical is known about them; and in the second place, because the genesis of Islam is rationally explained in the Qur'an itself for our enlightenment. The Qur'an, be it remembered, is a revelation to man through the mind of a man to whom it came as an inspiration of exalted and intelligible truths. To the recipient of the message the actual presence of an angel was as much an objective reality as his Daimon was to Socrates; to the modern rational mind it is some medium of communication more concrete than mere thought, a more vivid presentment to the senses which are impressed with its reality. Hence it is in the very nature of things that an angel 'appearing' to the 'inspired' person should remain invisible to all others not so inspired.

All the three Semitic religions inculcate belief in the existence of angels, their names, their functions and so on. Jews, Christians and Muslims all have to believe in them alike as Messengers of God's will.

God Revealed

The speculative wanderings of ancient philosophers in the region of the Infinite are referred to briefly but clearly in Cicero's Essay 'On the nature of the Gods'. In it we find that apart from the speculation to which philosophers had devoted themselves, there had always been a sort of vague belief in the minds of the Greeks and the Romans regarding the existence of God, and that this fact itself was used by some philosophers as the strongest argument to prove their existence. 'Since it is the constant and universal opinion of mankind independent of education, custom or law, there are Gods, it must necessarily follow that this knowledge is implanted in our minds or rather innate in us. That opinion respecting which there is a general argument in universal nature, must infallibly be true; then it must be allowed that there are Gods.' We, know how this kind of inferential belief lost all its vagueness and uncertainty in the Semitic mind and became a burning faith and took the form, in the case of the Prophets, of a God-directed impulse to proclaim itself to the world. This is what is meant by that inspiration which on account of its over-powering force and illuminating character is called Revelation.

The Unity of God in All Religions

All revealed religions known to us believe in the unity of God, in His omnipotence and benevolence, His justice and mercy; and all therefore enjoin man to be righteous in thought and deed. So far there is no essential difference in their teachings, and Moses and Jesus and Muhammad may be said to have held exactly the same creed in regard to the Deity and His commandments. Hence it would not be incorrect to say that the religion revealed through them is one and the same; and this is the truth on which the Qur'an insists. Believe in One God, it says, and follow the Right Path—which leads to Him. What is the right path? First of all, it is submission to His will as Master and Guide, then it is gratitude to Him for His bounty, and then it is the practice of righteousness in order to approach His presence. Do not all these conditions find their responsive counterpart in that faculty of the human soul to which we give the name 'conscience'? Though they come to us as religious commandments, they are not extraneous to us—they are the common ground on which religion and philosophy come into vital contact with our own inner nature and its aspirations. The Qur'an like other revelations only serves to establish and strengthen this contact.

Qur'an an Intelligible Message

When reading the Qur'an, it would be well to remember that if God spoke to man, He would have to do so in man's language in order to be understood, and He would have to reduce the ideas and concepts contained in His message to the measure of man's intelligence and capacity; and that the imagery used would be such as to appeal to man's understanding. The soul of man which is the receiver of messages, is never constrained by Him to carry a burden it cannot bear, or to receive a message it cannot understand, for that would be a tyranny for which there is no room in the divine order of things. Would it not therefore, be right to conclude that it would obviously be outside the scope of divine intention to convey to man intimations of eternal truths in language that man was incapable of understanding, or in mere abstractions, or in such propositions as only the trained intellect of a professor of metaphysics could hope to master? We might well imagine the Almighty communicating abstruse philosophic messages to a Plato, or profound problems of theology to a Milton; but we cannot bring ourselves to believe that He would adopt the same method when addressing untutored minds for the purpose of guiding them on the straight path of moral conduct.

In view of all this we have to admit that in its appeal to unprejudiced minds the convincing power of the Qur'an lies in its simple reasonableness; because there is an instinctive correspondence between the rational mind and truth, independent of faith or enforced credulity.

The reasonableness of the Qur'an

And in this way people of other persuasions who approach the Qur'an as a human document produced by a sincere highly-wrought mind in a mood of uncommon exaltation, can easily examine and appreciate its merits on intelligible grounds.

It is a fact never to be forgotten that this Revelation was given to the world through the medium of a human mind, in language that can be easily understood by man, and as easily applied to his needs. The central principle upon which it insists is the absolute oneness of the Creator of the universe—a principle already recognized by philosophy and reason ages ago. From this principle, it proceeds to explain the relation subsisting between the Creator and His creation culminating in man. It demands that man shall admit this relationship, rise in spirit to adore his Creator and make his own actions conform to the highest standard of purity and righteousness; thus only can he fulfil the essential conditions of the divine relationship. In this demand, obviously, there is no compulsion except that of reason; no mystery, no abstruse doctrine and no strained effort of faith involved. Faith is invited to admit the supreme authority of an Omnipotent, Omniscient, Omnipresent supervising Power, and here again faith is supported by reason, for the inter-connection of all created objects, whatever their forms and their position in the general scheme, whatever their connection with the central creative force or will from which they emanate, is as much a postulate of science as it is an article of faith. Science, examining nature piecemeal by a slow and laborious process, arrives successively at isolated fragments of the great truth, whereas faith with its inner illumination takes immediate cognizance of it and leaps to it by a spontaneous impulse. When the question of revelation is considered in this aspect, all revelations vouchsafed to fervent and sincere minds become equally true as facts, and any theory of deliberate imposture may be assigned without hesitation to ignorance or to the impotent malice of prejudiced minds. It is only the tolerant mind that can see the truth as it is, as it is only the intolerant mind that imagines its own preconceptions to represent the truth. The Qur'an readily accepts all previous Revelations as true and enjoins belief in them; and what it condemns in those who have accepted those Revelations is merely the infringement of the divine commandments communicated to them. And, further, it points out clearly that punishment shall be meted out to them, not because they are followers of other dispensations, but because they have distorted their original meaning and violated their spirit. Where the principles of revealed religions have been overlaid with the doctrines of dogmatic theology in the course of many centuries, as history shows, this charge cannot easily be refuted.

CHAPTER IV

The Scope of the Qur'an

The Morality of the Qur'an

TO a modern reader there is nothing so striking in the Qur'an as its insistence on practical righteousness. Doing right together with belief in God and in the Prophet's mission, is the underlying principle of Islam. Those who believe in God and at the same time practice righteousness may be said to *earn* salvation. This has been made quite clear in many passages scattered throughout the book, where the word 'earn' has actually been used. We arrive at the essential condition, righteousness in all the affairs of life, by putting together all the injunctions and prohibitions and explanations contained in it.

In examining the standard of morality given in the Qur'an we may at once dismiss from our minds such questions as that of polygamy, because this is not essentially a question of morality. The injunction that we must restrain our passions belongs to the domain of ethics, and is substantially the same in the Qur'an as in the maxim: virtue lies in the mean. The Qur'an condemns all excess leading to transgression. This is one of the principles on which it insists.

Besides scattered passages relating to morality, there are to be found in some chapters fairly comprehensive lists of the qualities constituting Islamic righteousness. These can be easily arranged in their proper order so that a correct idea may be formed of the ethical teachings of the Qur'an.

This will show how many injunctions of a moral nature are to be found in the Holy Book, which may be said to be our code of ethics—purity of heart and righteousness, contentment and gratitude to God, truthfulness and sincerity, justice and mercy, benevolence and beneficence, honesty and integrity, obedience to parents and to those in righteous authority, unselfishness and sympathy, kindness and charity, and above all, temperance and moderation to make these qualities active and effective. Followers of other religions, whether they believe in the divine origin of the Qur'an, or not, must admit that it is far more complete as a guide to conduct and far more lucid and far more effective in directing human conscience than any other ancient code that has come down to us. No Lawgiver of the past (no shadowy Solon or Lycurgus) has given us half as much, and no Plato or Aristotle has given us more in the way of clear rules for the conduct of life. What is most remarkable in these injunctions is that they breathe a spirit that acts with electric swiftness and potency to thrill the heart. There is a subdued fervour in them that burns its way to the very soul of the hearer through the homely garb of speech in which they are clothed. Marvellous was the effect it produced upon the heart of the unsophisticated Arab of the desert in the seventh century; it electrified him, it transformed him, till from the grovelling posture of an unclean animal wallowing in filth, he sprang to the height of heroic and saintly manhood within the space of a single life-time, and felt himself ordained to guide other nations. Marvellous! This is the miracle of miracles worked by the Prophet.

Nation building

We prate of nation-building now. Just think how the Arab nation was 'built' in the seventh century by the breath of one middle-aged man inspired by the Qur'an, within a period of less than twenty-five years!

The Qur'an led him, and he led his nation along the path of moral consciousness to an overpowering sense of human responsibility to God, the Creator and Judge. And this responsibility included the duty of carrying God's message to the remotest quarters of the earth. It included also, as a necessary consquence, the endeavour to overcome all obstacles to its success. A careful reading of those 'ayats' of the Qur'an in which battles and warlike operations are mentioned convinces us that it was not for territorial expansion that the Arabs were exhorted to go forth to meet nations more powerful than themselves, but to invite them to Islam as the natural religion of all! There are passages which support this view; and there are some 'ayats' which to me are like windows opening out on the expanding scene of Islamic history. As I dwell over them my mental vision seems to spread out, and I follow it as an eager spectator from the miniature battles of Ohud and Badr to the grand national campaigns in Syria and in Persia, in Egypt and in Spain—all for making the Truth prevail.

Qur'an as Hikmat, Philosophy

The Qur'an claims to be Hikmat (philosophy), but it is not a treatise on Ethics or on Metaphysics. It claims to be Haq (truth) but it is not an essay or a dissertation on Truth. It gives us the essence of Ethics in terse phrases scattered throughout its pages.

The Qur'an may not be an artistic, well arranged composition, judged by the standard of the West; but we must not forget that it does not claim to be a work of art; neither is it a composition. As we have already pointed out in the previous chapter, it is a series of messages, directions, commandments literally thrown out—coming through a fervent mind that was

God-possessed. The mind which received and the mouth which uttered the words were only passive instruments. That which threw them up was an irresistible force—so overpowering that the recipient appeared to be in a 'fit' while it lasted. This was the method, and this was the machinery. Now let us see whether they give us truth, goodness, purity, righteousness as the aim and object of man's life, or falsehood and improbability.

The word 'Hikmat' (Philosophy) has been used in the Qur'an as an epithet characterising the import of its teachings, and it is a true epithet. The Qur'an gives the essence of philosophy and puts the fervour of life into it. This philosophy rises above the sphere of metaphysical speculation and passes into the region of spiritual certainty. It grasps the truth after which metaphysical systems are still groping in the dark after a vain search extending over many centuries. It does not make any vain efforts to reach the Absolute—it finds God. And, more than this, it shows us the way to find Him. The approach indicated by it is at first through physical Nature—the domain of science. It exhorts us to look round and see and understand how Nature's forces are working, and to consider what Power could have made the earth and the skies and all that they contain. It enjoins us also to consider who could have made man from a small life-germ, who has made Life and Death, and who has the power to convert the one into the other. All these are legitimate enquiries for science so far as apparent cause and effect are concerned; but science comes to a standstill at the point where the question is 'Who made it thus?' At this point, where metaphysical philosophy is impotent to give a direct answer, the Qur'an, in the name of religion, boldly declares God to be the Author. It does not resort to any such subterfuge as Cosmic Will or First Cause! It puts life into the abstractions of philosophy and makes them culminate in the Godhead, giving personality to the Absolute!

God is perpetually manifesting Himself to man through His creation, He has no need to reduce Himself to a man or to a man-made image in order to assert His divinity with effect. The Qur'an reminds man of this fact, strikes at the root of idolatry and abolishes gross anthropomorphism.

In this supreme sense it is Hikmat—reason and truth blending with faith. It is living, not dead, philosophy.

Amidst our world environments, do we not hold a position that may be said to be relative to them all? Perhaps our relativity goes further; we are related to all that was, and all that is, and all that shall be for ever and ever! An idea that fills us with awe and a truth from which there is no escape; we remain imprisoned in it.

Man in Creation

Is our soul then, we ask, tied to the triumphal car of a blind universe to be dragged along with it back into nothingness or is it a well-adjusted, beautiful part of a grand and beautiful scheme which will go on perpetually evolving into something grander and more beautiful still? We have to believe this and hope that as there is a sensuous world of beauty here to gratify our senses so will there be elsewhere a spiritual world of beauty to gratify the purer longing of the disembodied spirit. And if the shadow-senses left to us as a part of our 'self' require it, there may be for our spirit two separate worlds of beauty—one a seemingly sensuous, and the other a purely spiritual one. Our conception of paradise comes very near to this, and its accepted imagery can be explained in this way.

Through Nature lies our way to God. Instinct first and then thought following a process of deduction tells us that a Reality, a creative Power is moulding and shaping and controlling the Universe and regulating its modes of operation. Thus do we arrive at the conception of a Creator and a Lawgiver; and at this point science, the result of observation, and faith the consummation of an inborn instinct seem to meet and emerge as religion.

Some such process as this is indicated by the Qur'an which constantly directs man's attention to the works of God and their suggestive power. Many are the passages in which the various aspects of Nature's work are appealed to, and all for the purpose of confirming the central creed—the unity and supremacy of the Creator. He is the Maker of the earth and skies and all that is contained in them. He is the Controller of all things, and all things issue from Him and all things return to Him. He has but to say to a thing 'Be' and it is. He creates man from a small drop of moisture, forms his flesh and blood and bone and muscle, and makes life reside in them; and in that life he puts an inner life, the soul, which is ultimately made independent of the external frame. This soul is endowed with thought and reason and judgment, and has the power to control the actions of the body. It is also made to feel its affinity with the powers of God and has a constant upward tendency which impels it to seek its Maker. It is to this tendency in man that the Qur'an addresses itself, and it is to the suppression of it by the misdirected will of man that it gives the name of 'Kofr' or denial, which is condemned as a falsehood.

All this seems to be in accord with what we call 'reason'; and surely reason is no other than correct judgment of the inter-relation of things.

Religion and Philosophy

Religion contains the essence of philosophy, but expresses it in a different manner and presents its concepts in a more concrete form. It can rise to the highest conception of the Universe without losing itself in the metaphysical inane. The metaphysical idea of God can only be reached by a process of negation of attributes, for the Absolute must be unqualified. In the words of a well known writer 'To think of the deity you must think of it as neither here nor there, then or now, you must be away with all limitations of time and space and matter, nay, with the very conditions, the limitations of thought itself', 'Apparently not observing that to think of it in this way was in reality not to think of it at all—that in short being so pure as this is pure nothing.' (Walter Pater *Plato and Platonism.*)

In this way we reach what some of the ancient Greek philosophers called the One, Being, and so on.

The human mind without going so far as to create the deity in its own image may yet require for its worship an intelligible God, one who, besides being capable of being conceived by it in some way or other should possess the power of satisfying its needs, and should, moreover, have those attributes which the human mind regards as best in itself. Such a God, all-powerful, all-knowing, all-wise, beneficent and just, Islam proclaims to man. In spite of His eternity and infinity and ubiquity, His oneness and His absoluteness, He is to the mind of man not a pure Nothing, but a Being who controls, and beneficently controls the universe and the heart of man.

If there is any anthropomorphism involved in this conception it is inevitable both to man and to the God whom alone man can worship. So much of anthropomorphism is indispensable in order to vivify the Absolute for the needs of man; and religion would be purposeless and meaningless if it did not bring God and man into intimate relationship. Its primary function is to do this, and the various religions of the world have done it, well or ill.

We must never forget that the idea of personal relation and personal contact with God is dear to the human heart, and without it there can be no religion at all. Taking these facts as they are, we are led to certain inferences which also have to be taken into account in treating of religion generally and of any given religion in particular. To satisfy the human mind the moral attributes of a living God must be truth, goodness, justice and mercy. From these flows as a direct consequence, the idea of reward and punishment, of heaven and hell. Man cannot free his mind from this unless he does away with the idea of God and His power and becomes an atheist. If there is to be a meting out of reward and punishment, there must be a judgment and a time for it, and there must also be a conceivable place or state of pleasure or pain to which the judged must be assigned. Again, that state has to be conceivable by the mind of man; it must not be a mere philosophic negation. To say that to be evil is itself hell, and to be good is itself heaven—as a pedantic philosopher would say—is to mystify the human mind. Religion cannot adopt such language; it must present something concrete and definite to the mind and heart of man. The imagery of heaven and hell, as

Heaven and Hell

pictured by the Semitic religions, has incurred the scorn of philosophers on account of its sensuous presentation, but philosophers would do well not to overlook the fact that there can be no appeal to the common mind except through the senses. If man were told that heaven meant a state of bliss, what would this convey to his mind, however philosophic that mind was? Does 'bliss' mean absence of pain, and pain, absence of bliss? A delightful circle of negation for the philosophic mind to perambulate in! Negative pain like this might frighten a philosopher, but it could not possibly impress the ordinary man. Pain therefore has to be presented as an unbearable torment to the imagination, and what can be more effective for this purpose than hell as an ever-blazing furnace? The scenery of heaven (as representing a state of bliss) is susceptible of more elaborate æsthetic treatment, and an artist's imagination would revel in the delight of investing it not only with all forms of beauty but with all the conditions that might appeal to all the senses. And the human mind is æsthetic—at least, potentially. But religion does not go into unnecessary details; it gives a simple but effective picture, suggestive of beauty and purity and peace. Heaven is pictured as a garden with streams flowing through it; it contains seats for the blest and beautiful crystal vessels are passed round in which there is a pure draught of celestial Bliss. There are also beautiful human-like forms, embodiments of beauty, for the blest to gaze upon. But with all this 'sensuous' bodying forth of beauty there is for the mind the constant spiritual occupation of adoring the all-perfect beauty and goodness of the Creator. In short, the human spirit has in the realms of Reality direct cognizance of what it once strove to apprehend dimly by efforts of imagination in the realm of earthly illusion. Thus there will be for it a continuity of imagination—a correspondence between its anterior imagination and present perception. Is this not the realm beyond which the sublimest effort of Plato's imagination could scarcely soar? Is it possible to conceive any other kind of heaven for it, when along with its 'survival' it must carry with it those faculties which make it what it is—a conscious soul?

The first instinctive movement of the human mind—or soul—is towards a personal, not an abstract God; and it is only afterwards as a result of deliberate questioning and by the employment of a dialectical process that man arrives at an abstraction—as Parmenides, for instance, arrived at his 'One'.

If the soul's return to its origin meant merely its remergence into the Universal soul, resulting in loss of identity and individuality, then it would be like a drop of water thrown back into the ocean, and immortality would mean nothing. But if on returning to its source it still carried with it any characteristic that could preserve its identity apart from other surrounding existences, then survival would be a reality and immortality a continuance of its former self in a gradually purified state, unhampered by the exactions of flesh and blood. This is how, religion teaches us, the human soul returns to God. There is no inconsistency between the different portions of the religious creed—between those relating to the soul's immortality and those relating to God's judgment and award. These are mutually adjustable links of the same chain of beliefs: they are, besides, links which can be reasonably argued and accepted by common intelligence. This is the main position taken up in the Qur'an, which exhorts man to understand and believe. The Qur'an gives us as a fact what philosophy has laboured for centuries to establish by reasoning.

There is a potent law of nature at work in what we call kinship and affinity, and there must be a faculty in the soul through which it operates. If we believe this to be true, then we must also believe that in the case of the soul surviving with all its faculties and with all those qualities which go to make up its individuality, this feeling of kinship and affinity and relationship will also go along with it into a future life, purged of its earthly and grosser characteristics.

Reunion in Heaven

A step further along this line of thought brings us nearer to the idea (or belief) that a realisation of that insistent feeling would be as necessary to its happiness in heaven as it ever was on earth. Another step, and we come to believe that heaven (which is to be a state of bliss) must provide full opportunity for such realisation. Thus we arrive at the belief that the disembodied spirit must be brought into contact and association with those whom it had loved on earth—father, mother, brother, sister, children, friends. And why not husband and wife? Divested of its grosser appetites, why should the soul not enjoy the happiness of realising its associations even in this case in a purer form? All religions, I believe, allow this, and the Qur'an is explicit in mentioning the fact. It refers (Ch. III, Sec. 2, cl. 14) to 'pure mates' in heaven after having mentioned in 13, man's desires in this world, viz., love of women, children, gold and silver, etc. And the 'pure mates' stand in marked contrast to objects of carnal desire. Why is there so much stress laid on the word 'pure'? This passage should always be borne in mind in connection with the heaven of Islam—which has been so vigorously assailed by the ignorant or malicious prejudice of writers who seem to carry their own pre-conceptions into the interpretation of passages in the Qur'an, the meaning of which is quite clear in the light of the verse mentioned above.

Now these 'pure mates' can either be the same earthly mates in their spiritualized and purified existence, or other pure spirits with whom there is 'affinity'. This brings us to the 'Hooris' referred to in some passages. Whatever these beings may be—mere women of the vulgar conception or an archetype of Beauty after the ideal of Plato's poetic philosophy—a visual presentation of the 'self-beautiful'—they are not provided as objects of sensuality in heaven! Such a supposition would be absurd in view of the purity which has been made an essential condition of life here and hereafter.

The 'Hoor' is a fine conception— finer than 'Angel'. No thin abstraction in descriptive phraseology could have presented to the imagination what was needed, and no sensuous presentation in a living spirit-world (where imagination is sensation), could have been possible in a less sensible form of beauty than this. The 'Hoor' is neither woman nor angel, but more beautiful than either; and the Hoor's function seems to be to gratify the love of the beautiful which, as one of the distinguishing attributes of the human soul, is innate in it. It represents in a form which is beyond our conception in this life what the mind of the Greek artist had an occasional glimpse of, and tried to reproduce in his art in the embodiment of ideal Beauty. Some might ask what justification is there for such an extraordinary interpretation? But what justification is there for putting the Hoor down as an ærial demi-monde? If anyone should find it possible to support such an interpretation as the latter, it might be inferred that his mind was not yet able to resist the fascination of carnal longings. Even supposing that such a conception of Hoor was an error of judgment, I would humbly submit that erring with Plato would be more like being on the way to heaven than adopting such a flesh-obsessed mentality as some writers have displayed!

CHAPTER V

The Aim of the Qur'an

'As one and the same universal nature unites and corroborates all the parts of the world, so did she unite into one harmonious family all mankind. But men through their depravity disagreed and quarrelled, not recollecting that they are all consanguineous and akin, and equally subject to the same paternal providence. If this fact, indeed, were but kept in mind, all men might live the amiable life of the gods.'

Mankind one Nation

Thus wrote Cicero two thousand years ago, and the Qur'an purporting to make mankind one nation, righteous and strong, announced the fact in plain words more than thirteen hundred years ago. And we are still dreaming that the whole of mankind might be one race and one united nation!

Is this not still a dream, and are we not talking about it as though we were in earnest and meant to make it come true? Will any League of Nations succeed in achieving this end? What do all our Peace Conferences, and all our offers of disarmament really signify? Our efforts may be sincere; but unfortunately they seem to be confined to merely external conditions and do not penetrate down to those vital conditions which lie at the heart of human affairs; and certainly they do not aim with any degree of sincerity at removing the internal causes of disharmony and dissension. Our minds are still obsessed with age-long ingrained prejudices relating to religion and nationality and country and commercial interests, and we are

The Disease

either powerless or unwilling, in spite of all our protestations, to remove these barriers which prevent us from meeting on the common ground of humanity. We still adhere to geographical demarcations to which we have attributed greater national significance by falsely persuading ourselves that they correspond to certain mental and moral types which themselves connote qualities of superiority and inferiority. Is not the dictum 'East is east and West is west' supposed to contain the quintessence of international wisdom and political prudence?

While professing to recognise the sanctity of geographical boundaries, do we not forget or ignore the lesson of history, which is ever busy upsetting those boundaries? Conquerors have delighted in making new geography, and history has followed in the wake of their triumphs diligently registering their exploits and re-mapping the earth. When Europe represented by the Roman Eagles overleapt its borders and treated Africa and Egypt and Syria and Palestine and Arabia Felix as apanages of Rome and part and parcel of the Roman Empire; and when Asia as represented by the faith of Islam and Arab prowess, made nearly all those portions of the nerveless Roman Empire the subject-domain of Arabia, what became of geographical limits then; and what has become of them under the world domination of the greatest Empire of modern times? They were conventions, and have been treated as such and have given way to other conventions. But the one great and desirable convention that all mankind shall be one nation, has yet to gain due recognition.

There has been so much confounding of geographical boundaries and so much interfusion of races and customs and manners, and even of faiths and beliefs in this world during the period known to history that the fact of humanity remaining still cooped up in certain conventional compartments is surprising. It stands before our eyes an undeniable fact, and the more we wish to ignore it the greater grows its tyranny over our hidden feelings. Does not the European still think of the Asiatic as being distantly, and in a figurative sense, his brother, while the brown or yellow colour of the brother's skin, his different religion, and his uncivilized ways and a crowd of differentiating sentiments causing repugnance rush into his mind and make it a soil where fraternal sympathy cannot thrive? The European's natural bias, which makes him cling to certain inherited or traditional notions regarding religion and civilization and morality and human capability, tends rather to accentuate the difference between himself and others in these respects than to mitigate them through finer feeling, by making due allowance for their accidental existence. Similarly, the Asiatic too has his own prejudices and obsessions; and being, admittedly, more backward cannot get rid of his cruder mentality and consequent narrowness of vision and sympathy. Islam boldly abolishes these distinctions and differences by proclaiming THE QUALITY OF MAN.

The Remedy
1. Unity of God, Rallying point for all

We observe the existing symptoms of the disease; and Islam shows the remedy: a changed outlook in which there shall be no place for any of the old superstitions and prejudices! And the first step towards this must be the simplification and purification of our religious creeds. The central creed of course must be the unity of God, the source of all being. This is the only belief that can be supported and strengthened by reason and philosophy, and the only belief which is actually enshrined in all religions. Hence there should be no difficulty in the way of educated people to accept it as the common ground on which all can and must meet. It follows from this that all those superstitions and prejudices must be discarded which find their sustenance in mysteries and sacraments, themselves the creatures of priestcraft and dogmatic theology.

Remedy: Common. 2. Respect for Founders of Religions

Polytheism, as we know, likes to take shelter behind the explanation that the great God being one, all other accepted deities are merely manifestations of His different attributes and powers. We may accept this explanation as sincere, but, at the same time, the so-called polytheist might be persuaded that the abstract notion of the one supreme God is a purer, higher, and nobler conception than that of a multiplicity of subordinate and inferior deities—whether they be regarded as mere manifestations and emanations or as separate independent existences. So far the difficulty is not insuperable; but when we come to the question of the divine mission of those great men who brought the different religions into the world, the force of long existing associations and, possibly, the inveteracy of certain prejudices born of them, will present serious obstacles. But let us hope that a spirit of toleration fostered and strengthened by proper education and aided by a spirit of reverence for the high station and the benefactions of those who have been the guides of mankind on the path of faith and righteousness, will in due course enable the mind to overcome these obstacles. There is no doubt that the world has benefited by the teachings of many prophets and sages through a long series of centuries; and that each one of them has rendered some service to the great cause of human regeneration. It should not therefore be difficult for enlightened minds to give to their memories the praise and reverence due. The followers of the Mosaic, the Christian and the Islamaic dispensations find the ground already prepared, and they have only to broaden their views a little and forget their past quarrels. They believe in and serve the same God, and they received the same light from Him in the same region of the earth by means of prophets belonging to the same race, and each of those prophets believed in the divine mission of his predecessors and reverenced them as God's chosen messengers. Here is enough common ground on which to meet; and if we could remove the mass of prejudices which have grown round the pure faith, and do away with most of those observances which are no more than mere ritual, our path will be made smoother still. Religion after all, in the eyes of cultured people, is only morality made sublime by faith; and in this view of it all can readily unite. And this is the teaching of Islam.

The notion has become current that some religions have condemned other religions in harsh terms, and even gone so far as to exclude their followers from the benefit of God's mercy and salvation. I am inclined to doubt the truth of this. So far as I have been able to understand those passages of the Qur'an in which punishment is threatened to persistent unbelievers, it is only the refusal to believe in the unity of God and in the object of the mission of his Apostles which is condemned. This is quite logical, for he who does not believe in the one supreme God, does not believe in His justice and in His mercy, and therefore deliberately excludes himself from the benefit of these attributes. Can he consistently claim any right under a jurisdiction to which he does not submit himself?

In the 20th century when even the commonest civilized being scorns crass idolatry and considers only one God as possible, his faith, such as it may be, must naturally centre in one God alone. In this way the more serious aspect of denial has become almost impossible in these days. And as regards belief in the divine mission of prophets and religious guides, no one who is acquainted with the miraculous effects of their teachings in 'uplifting' degenerate peoples can possibly deny their mission as an accomplished fact. Their's has been the most successful mission in the world, and to those whose faith in any movement depends on its success, this should be a sufficient argument. And to those who take sincerity to be the real test of truth in man no other argument seems necessary than the spirit of these guides as revealed in their work. It was the God-possessed spirit in them, provocative almost of martyrdom, that proclaimed the truth of their mission. On these purely rational grounds I am convinced that there is as little difficulty in acknowledging the greatness and sanctity of all the spiritual guides who have appeared in the world from time to time as there is in accepting the supremacy of the one God. This is the central creed of the Qur'an, and it was to invite mankind to accept it, that the Arab went forth into the world.

Islam not 'Militant'

I have little doubt that the truth-loving mind of modern Europe will in course of time feel strongly attracted by what it has hitherto misunderstood and maligned. It will realise that Islam is not a 'militant faith' though it had to fight in self-defence. It was Gibbon's love of the picturesque in the pageant of history that tempted him to use the expression 'Sword in one hand and Qur'an in the other'. He as historian of the decline of the Roman Empire had to face the fact which stood out more prominently than any other in the 7th century A.D.—namely, the rise of the Muslim power on the borders of the Eastern Roman Empire. The plain Arab of the desert who confronted the well-armed, well-accoutred Roman legionary was indeed a strange phenomenon. He had the Qur'an (newly given to him) not only in his hand but in his heart, and the sword had always been his inseparable companion. It was very natural for him to travel through life with these two gifts—and to use them as his sense of right dictated. As it happened, he came up against great powers representing ancient civilizations, and his instinct enabled him to see through their gorgeous semblance—to detect their internal decay and to realise his own growing strength. He touched them and they crumbled to pieces! But mark! he did not force the Qur'an on them at the point of his sword; he merely said that if they chose to adopt his faith they would be his brethren. At the same time he made it quite clear to them that if they chose to fight he on his part was quite ready to fight. He made it equally clear that if they did not choose to fight but acknowledged themselves his 'tributaries' they would have to pay so much 'tribute' every year and would be left unmolested under his protection. He left their religion alone; he had nothing to do with it. This is history, whatever prejudiced anti-Islamic writers may say to the contrary. Gibbon himself has quoted numerous instances of the humanity (and even gentleness) of the Arabs in their dealings with other nations, which so impressed the Romans that some of the highest dignitaries among them—Romanus, Governor of Basra, for example—voluntarily embraced Islam. Both Ockley and Gibbon themselves are sufficient as witnesses against 'the Qur'an and the Sword' calumny.

The Heroes of Islam

Islamic history as every one knows, is rich in episodes of heroism and chivalry, and presents a wonderful spectacle of united national action under the influence of a spirit born of unwavering faith in the immediate guidance of an all-seeing and all-directing beneficent Power. Islam generated an impulse that created heroes and so directed it that they soon made a nation of heroes! There is nothing like it in the history of any other nation or country. The first century of Islam comprises within its narrow limits the rise of a new power and a new empire and a new civilization. Innumerable events of stupendous magnitude and importance, and of epic interest, are spread over it, besides which many Iliads and Aeneiids would sink into insignificance. It is too vast a theme for one epic—it is a congeries of a great number of splendid epics, the subject of each of which is the birth of a great State as the outward symbol of a great Faith. The Iliad treats of the destruction of the town of Troy by the united armies of the several States and Kingdoms of Greece, and the whole action is focussed in the arrogant valour of Achilles and the self-devoting heroism of Hector. But the greatness of the Islamic epic and the magnificence of the exploits of its heroes are such that the personal triumphs of the Conquerors of Persia and Syria and Egypt and Africa and Spain are only recalled as half-forgotten details of a new World-movement! Indeed, they were regarded by the people of the age in which they were performed as no more than mere performance of duty by true-hearted Muslims whose hands could over-turn kingdoms and yet whose hearts were capable of unparalleled self-effacement. Such was the effect of the Qur'anic teaching.

Islam the religion of the brave

In my view the essential qualities of Islam make it the religion of the brave: its stern self-denial supported by a scorn of the things of this world; its calm fortitude born of an unquestioning trust in, and absolute dependence on an unseen God for whose worship no visible symbols are needed; its sober hopefulness which leaves no room for disappointment or dejection; its serene resignation to the will of a just and beneficent Power; its unwavering faith in a scheme of universal life resting ultimately on Good. A true follower of Islam has his God always with him and is therefore afraid of nothing. He can suffer no loss because he does not prize anything but the approbation of his Creator. He is not afraid of death because he looks upon it as the entrance to a higher life that takes him nearer to the divine presence. He is taught to believe that as all good comes from God, so all evil comes from the misdirection of man's own faculties. He believes also that Good will conquer Evil as surely as Truth will conquer Falsehood. Evil for him has no separate existence, it is only a deviation from good. Under the misguiding influence of his own passions, man is led to the pursuit of objects that in themselves have no permanence. With his better judgment to guide him, he is always in a penitential

آية

mood, and seeking to emerge from it purified and exalted in spirit. Suffering to him is a trial along the path which leads to God, and if death lies at the end of his earthly career of suffering, it lies also at the end of his earthly career of enjoyment: it is the entrance through which he must pass on his way to a higher life. And man thus purified and strengthened can become an efficient instrument of God's will for carrying on the work of life.

This is the philosophy of life taught us by the Qur'an. And is not this—though somewhat differently expressed—the ultimate belief of all ethical philosophies and almost all religions?

But the Qur'an does not leave the matter at that. Thought must be wrought into belief, and belief must be energized into emotion which must find expression in *action*. This was the natural process by which the Qur'an and its exponent wrought the splendid miracle of Islamic history.

The Qur'an teaches man how to become Invincible by faith and righteous endeavour; and the whole career of the Prophet illustrates this lesson.